creatures of the sea

Sponges

Kris Hirschmann

KIDHAVEN PRESS
An imprint of Thomson Gale, a part of The Thomson Corporation

Detroit • New York • San Francisco • San Diego
New Haven, Conn. • Waterville, Maine • London • Munich

For more information, contact
KidHaven Press
27500 Drake Rd.
Farmington Hills, MI 48331-3535
Or you can visit our Internet site at http://www.gale.com

LIBRARY OF CONGRESS CATALOGING-IN-PUBLICATION DATA

Sponges / by Kris Hirschmann, 1967–.
p. cm. — (Creatures of the sea)
Includes bibliographical references and index.
ISBN 0-7377-3013-7 (hard cover : alk. paper)
1. Sponges—Juvenile literature. I. Title.
QL371.6.H57 2005
593.4—dc22

2004022746

Printed in the United States of America

Table of Contents

Introduction

Simple Survivors

People have known about sponges for thousands of years. For most of this time, however, no one knew whether sponges were plants or animals. It was not until the early 1800s that scientists discovered that sponges eat bits of **organic** matter, as animals do, rather than taking in chemicals for survival, as plants do. Scientists also learned that sponges breathe oxygen, like animals, rather than carbon dioxide, like plants. And finally, they found that sponges actively pumped water through their bodies—something a plant could not do. These traits proved once and for all that sponges were indeed animals.

Animals they may be, but there is no question that sponges are very *unusual* animals. These creatures do

Although these colorful tube sponges might look like exotic underwater plants, they are actually living, breathing animals.

not always have a set shape or size. They have no organs of any sort—no brain, heart, eyes, stomach, or any of the other features most animals have. They have no circulatory systems. They also have no nerves, which means they basically have no senses. In short, sponges are incredibly simple creatures that do very little other than sit in one place and survive.

Simple but Successful

Despite their simplicity, sponges are among the world's most successful animals. The fossil record shows that sponges have been on Earth for at least 550 million years—longer than almost any other type of creature. And they are just as plentiful in modern times as ever. Today sponges thrive in every ocean and sea around the world. These animals are living proof that a big brain and other fancy features are not necessary for survival. In the ocean, as in life, the simple way sometimes turns out to be the best.

chapter 1

Pores and More

When people think of sponges, they usually imagine the soft, hole-filled objects used for bathing and cleaning. These objects, however, are not really sponges. A true sponge is a living animal that makes its home in the ocean. Natural bath sponges are the dried and bleached skeletons of these animals.

Scientists believe that there are between 15,000 and 20,000 species of sponges. Of these, about 5,500 species have been described so far. All sponges belong to the scientific phylum **Porifera**. This name comes from Latin words that mean "bearing pores." It is a good description of the sponge, which is covered with pores of many sizes. These openings lead into a body filled with thousands of canals, passages,

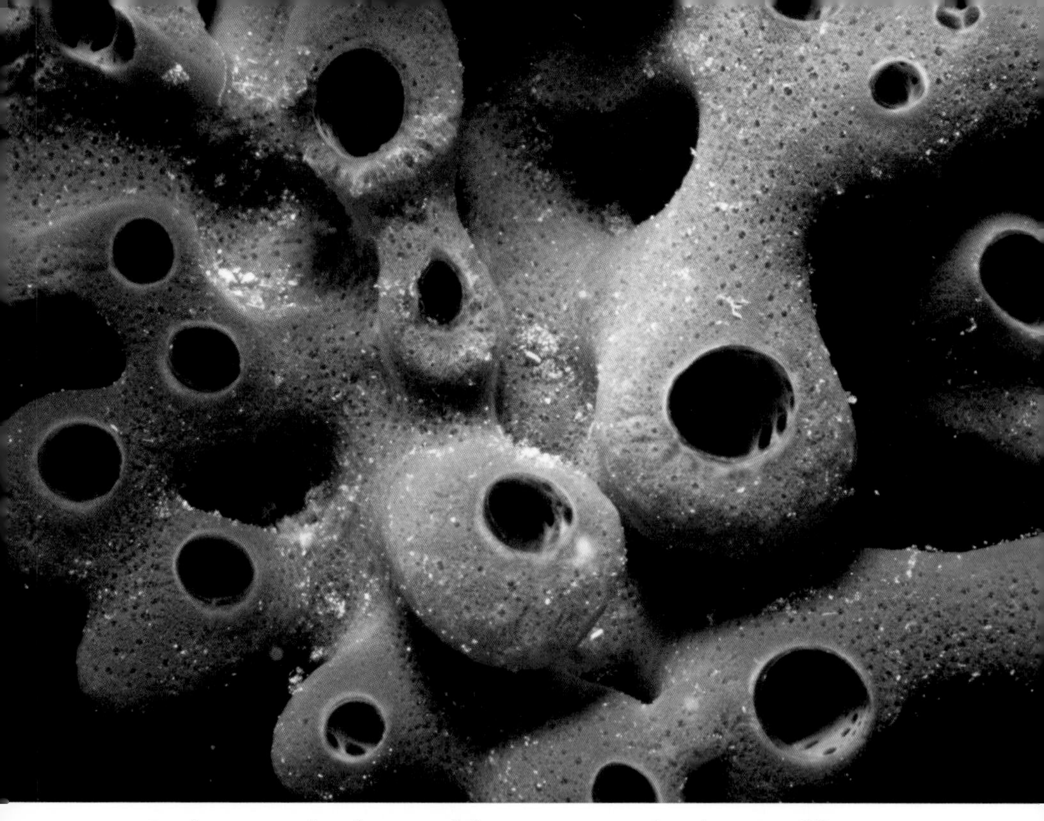

A close-up look at a blue sponge in the Pacific Ocean shows the thousands of pores that cover its surface.

and chambers. With all these openings and cavities, the sponge's body is a lot like a living sieve or filter.

Where Sponges Live

Although there are some freshwater sponges, the vast majority of sponge species live in salt water. These animals are found in all of the world's oceans and seas, from the warm regions near the equator to the freezing areas around the poles. They are especially common in the waters of the Caribbean, Mexico, Japan, California, and the Gulf of Mexico near Florida. Huge numbers of sponges also live in the Red Sea and the Mediterranean Sea. Sponges can be found at all depths, from tidal regions to the ocean floor more than 4 miles (6.4km) deep.

Sponges spend their whole lives in one place, anchored to a solid surface. For this reason, they usually live in places with plenty of hard materials to which they can attach themselves. In shallow tropical waters, for example, sponges are most often found on coral reefs. They are especially common at the lower levels of the reef. In reefless waters, sponges are usually found in rocky areas. Underwater mountains and ridges are especially good growing areas for sponges.

These orange stove-pipe sponges are firmly anchored to a coral reef in the Caribbean Sea.

Sponges do not usually settle in flat areas, which tend to be covered with a layer of silt that makes it hard for sponges to attach themselves. Some species, however, have found a way around this problem. These sponges grow a long, thin stalk into the soft sediment of the sea floor. The body of the sponge, which is connected to the top of the stalk, floats a short distance above the bottom. It is securely attached by its slender anchor.

Identifying Sponges

Sponges come in a huge range of sizes. Large species, such as the coral reef tube sponges, can grow as tall as a person. The barrel sponge, which is shaped like its name, may be so big that a diver can comfortably sit inside its central opening. These creatures, however, are the giants of the sponge world. Most species are much smaller, and some grow no bigger than kernels of corn.

Shape, too, is very different from species to species. Some sponges are nearly round, while others are branched, hairy, or irregular. Many sponges grow upward from a small attachment area, while others spread like a crust over the surrounding rocks and coral. Shapes can sometimes be used to identify a sponge species. But this technique can be tricky, since local conditions change the way a sponge grows. A sponge in an area with strong currents, for example, may grow differently than a sponge of the same species in calm water. So shape is not always a good clue to a sponge's identity.

A diver in the Caribbean Sea holds a giant barrel sponge, one of the world's largest sponges.

Identification by color can be hard as well. Sponges come in all the shades of the rainbow, from yellow to green, blue to red, and every other hue in between. When taken out of the water, however, nearly all sponges lose their color. Without knowing what they looked like in their natural environment, it is very difficult to identify these bleached-out samples.

Because sponges can be so hard to identify by size, shape, and color, scientists use microscopes to look at the animals' internal features. The best way of identifying sponges is to look at structures within their

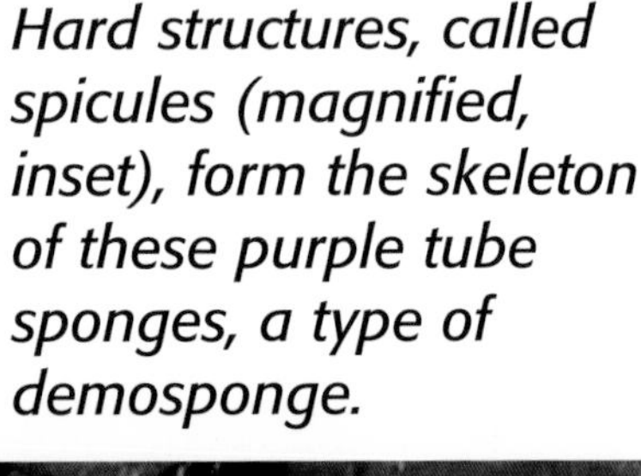

Hard structures, called spicules (magnified, inset), form the skeleton of these purple tube sponges, a type of demosponge.

bodies called **spicules**. Spicules come in a huge variety of shapes. They may be straight or curved, flat or fringed, and they may look like tiny spears, mushrooms, snowflakes, or countless other objects. Spicules are stacked or woven together to form a tough skeleton that surrounds and protects the sponge's cells.

Types of Sponges

Scientists recognize four types of sponges. The most common are the **demosponges**. About 80 percent of all known species fall into this category. Demosponges grow at all depths and in all temperatures. They have complex bodies filled with channels and tunnels. Some, such as the barrel sponges and the tube sponges, may grow very large. Most demosponges have spicules made of **silica**, which is a glasslike material. A few species do not have any spicules but instead have a skeleton made of **spongin**, a flexible substance similar to human hair and fingernails. Sponges with spongin skeletons are the ones used as bath sponges.

Like most demosponges, the **glass sponges** also have silica spicules. In the glass sponges, however, the spicules are always six-sided, like toy jacks. These spicules are woven together into a hard internal skeleton that supports the sponge's living cells. Glass sponges usually thrive in deeper waters, from about 700 feet (213m) below the sea surface to the darkest depths of the ocean. They are often found on the downward-sloping seafloor around continents. They are also common in deep waters near the Antarctic.

The **chalky sponges** make up the third major sponge family. These sponges have spicules made of a chalklike material called **calcium carbonate**. Chalky sponges tend to be small, growing to no more than 5 or 6 inches (13 to 15cm) in length. They live mostly on coral reefs and are seldom found in deep water.

There is a rare fourth family called the **hard sponges**. Hard sponges have glassy spicules and are covered by a thick, solid layer of calcium. They live in caves inside coral reefs and grow very slowly. A hard sponge that measures 12 inches (30cm) across may be thousands of years old.

Loosely Organized

Whatever family they belong to, all sponges' bodies work in a very unusual way. In most animals, cells are organized into larger structures (organs, bones, and so on) that perform certain functions. But the sponge's body is not organized in this way. A sponge is a loose collection of cells, each of which has an individual job to do. Some cells, for example, are shaped like hard plates and cover the outside of the sponge's body. Some pull water into the sponge, and some carry food and oxygen from place to place. Working on their own, the sponge's cells manage to do all the jobs necessary for their owner's survival.

A spiny sea star clings to an orange demosponge. The sponge's skeleton is made of flexible spongin (magnified, inset).

A sponge does not, however, have a brain or nerves to send information through the body. A sponge's cells do sense changing conditions, and they can send messages to each other by releasing chemicals. It takes a long time for these chemical messages to drift through the entire body, so sponges cannot react quickly to anything. But eventually all parts of the sponge will receive the information. The animal then begins to act. It may slowly tighten its pores, for example, if water conditions are rough, or it may start preparing to spawn as the ocean warms up in the summertime. Sponges even have special cells that can change into other kinds of cells if necessary. This ability helps sponges adjust when circumstances change. The adjustment happens very slowly—but it is fast enough to keep the sponge alive. And staying alive, after all, is the only thing that matters in the end.

chapter

2

Making New Sponges

Although different types of sponges have very different life spans, there is no question that sponges are among the longest-lived creatures on Earth. The hard sponges are known to live thousands of years, and sponges in other families can probably live for hundreds of years if conditions are favorable.

During its long life, a sponge's most important job is to create more sponges. Like all animals, sponges accomplish this job by reproducing. But unlike most creatures, a sponge has several ways to reproduce. By using the method that suits the circumstances, a sponge gives itself the best possible chance of survival.

During spawning season, an enormous basket sponge releases a cloud of sperm into the water.

Spawning

Many sea creatures—including sponges—reproduce by **spawning**, or releasing eggs and sperm into the water. Most sponges are able to make both eggs and sperm, which means they are not strictly male or female. But a sponge does not usually make both substances at the same time. When spawning season approaches, some sponges play the female role and form eggs. Others play the male role and form sperm. These sex roles can switch from season to season. A sponge that makes sperm one time, for example, may make eggs the next time spawning season arrives.

When conditions are just right, "male" sponges start to release sperm into the many water-filled channels inside their bodies. Currents carry the sperm out of the body in huge, smoky clouds. The clouds drift through the water until they are sucked in by a "female" sponge. Once inside the body, the sperm fertilizes the female's eggs. The material inside the eggs then begins to develop into sponge **embryos**.

At this point some demosponges release the fertilized eggs, which float for a short time before hatching in midwater. In most species, however, the eggs hatch into tiny **larvae** inside the mother's body. The outside of each larva's body is lined with little hairs, called **flagella**. The larva whips its flagella through the water to move itself around.

Sponge larvae live in the spaces between the mother sponge's cells until they are able to swim easily. Then they leave the mother's body through the pores and strike out on their own. A larva spends just a few hours or a day at most in the open water before settling to the seafloor. Once there, the larva attaches itself to a hard surface and begins to grow. In time the larva will turn into a mature sponge, able to spawn and create new larvae of its own.

Budding and Regeneration

Sponges can also reproduce by a method called **budding**. To bud, a sponge first grows branches off the main part of its body. Each branch is covered with pores, just like the parent sponge. It also contains the same types of cells and spicules as the parent. It has its own water circulation system. It is basically a whole new animal, still attached to its parent's body.

Sometimes a sponge's branches break off because of rough water, a predator, a kick from a careless diver, or another circumstance. When this happens, the branches are able to live on their own. A broken-off branch attaches itself to a hard surface as soon as it can. Then it starts to grow. Over time the new sponge gets bigger and bigger, and before long it is able to form branches of its own. These branches will eventually break off and create even more new sponges, thus continuing the cycle of life.

Similar to budding, sponges can also reproduce by a process called **regeneration**. Regeneration hap-

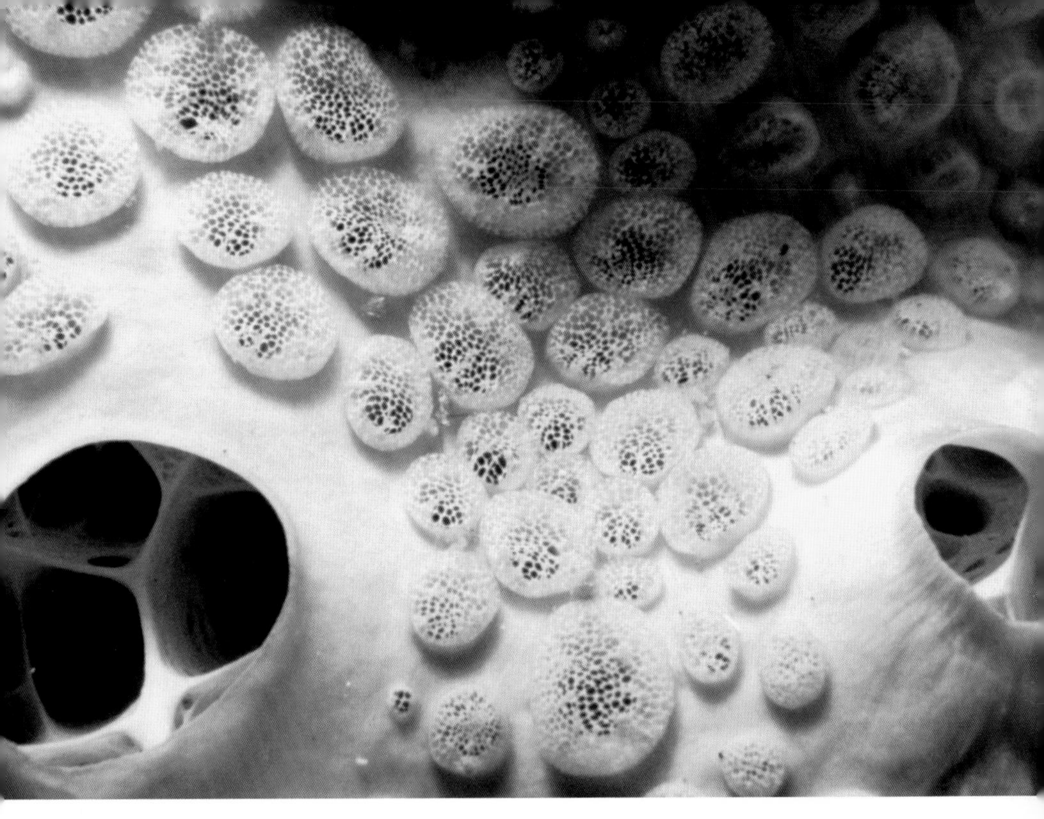

This sponge is reproducing by budding, a process in which new sponges grow from the parent's own body.

pens if a sponge gets broken into small pieces. The pieces are not as well developed as branches, and they may not have all the parts an adult sponge has. Still, they can survive if they manage to attach themselves to the seafloor. If conditions are good, the sponge bits quickly develop everything they need to grow and thrive in their new homes.

Surviving

Because sponges cannot move, they are at the mercy of their environment. Some sponges may enjoy good living conditions for hundreds of years. Others, however, may be affected by changes in their home areas. Water levels and temperatures can go up or down, for example, or food may begin to disappear. Near cities, pollution may poison the water. All of these changes can threaten a sponge's survival.

When conditions become unfavorable in these ways, a sponge activates its last—and most unusual—method of reproduction. The sponge starts to store food inside special cells in its body. These cells are then surrounded by other cells that build

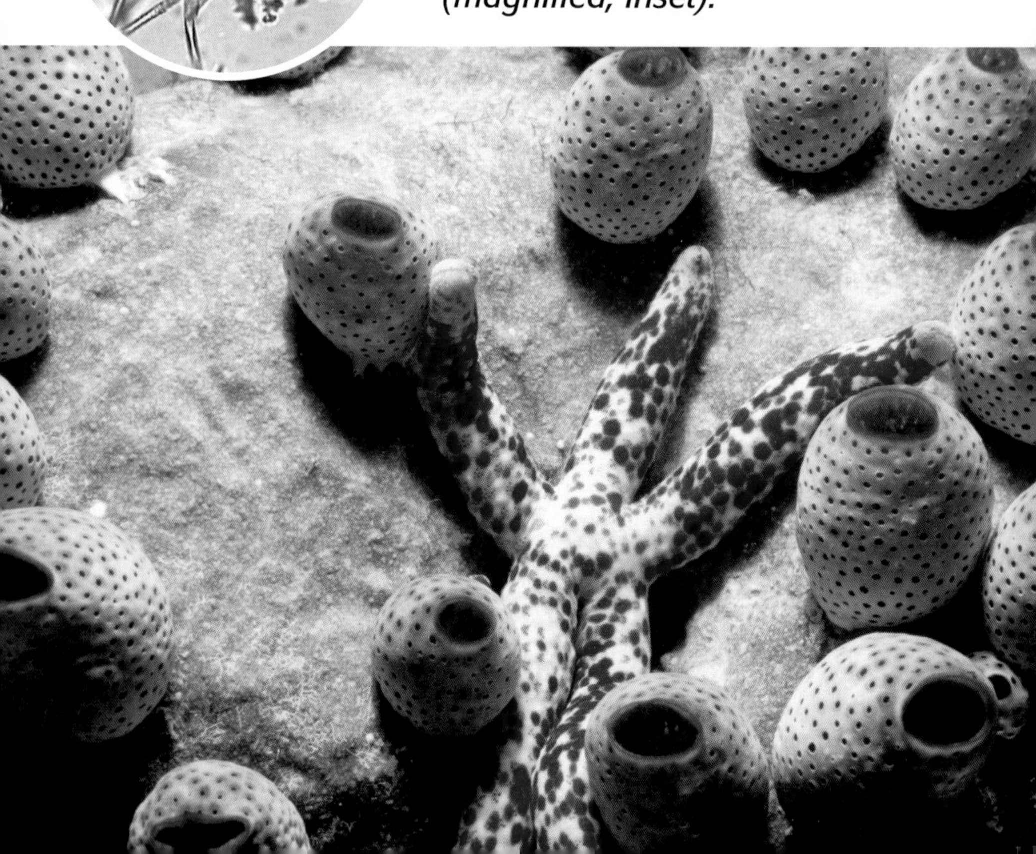

Sometimes sponges reproduce by releasing seedlike clusters of cells called gemmules (magnified, inset).

a hard coating of spongin and spicules. Eventually the original cells are completely buried in tough, round outer shells. These tiny structures are called **gemmules**, and a sponge may contain hundreds or even thousands of them. Each gemmule contains all the material necessary to create a new sponge. It is a lot like a seed, just waiting to be planted.

A New Generation

The gemmules sit inside the sponge's body as long as the sponge is alive. If the sponge dies, however, its living parts rot away, and the gemmules float into open water. Protected by their tough coverings, the gemmules can live through the same conditions that killed their parent. They drift freely with the ocean currents. After a while they may settle to the ocean floor in an area where conditions are better. When this happens, the gemmules break open. The food-filled cells inside the gemmule stream out and begin to build a new sponge.

Because conditions are slightly different from one part of the ocean to another, the new sponge will not look exactly like its dead parent. But at a cellular level, it is just the same. Sponges that grow from gemmules are clones of their parents. By creating gemmules, a sponge copies itself to create a new generation.

chapter 3

Sponges in the Food Chain

Like all living creatures, sponges must eat to survive. Almost all sponges are filter feeders, which means they eat by sifting food from the water. Single-celled bacteria and algae make good food for a sponge. So do tiny scraps of dead organic material from plants and animals. The oceans are full of these microscopic scraps, so a sponge usually finds all the food it needs.

Living Pumps

Before a sponge can eat, it must take in water and the food it contains from the ocean around it. The sponge's pore-filled body is perfectly designed for this task. A sponge draws water in through openings on the outside of its body. Inside the sponge, the water

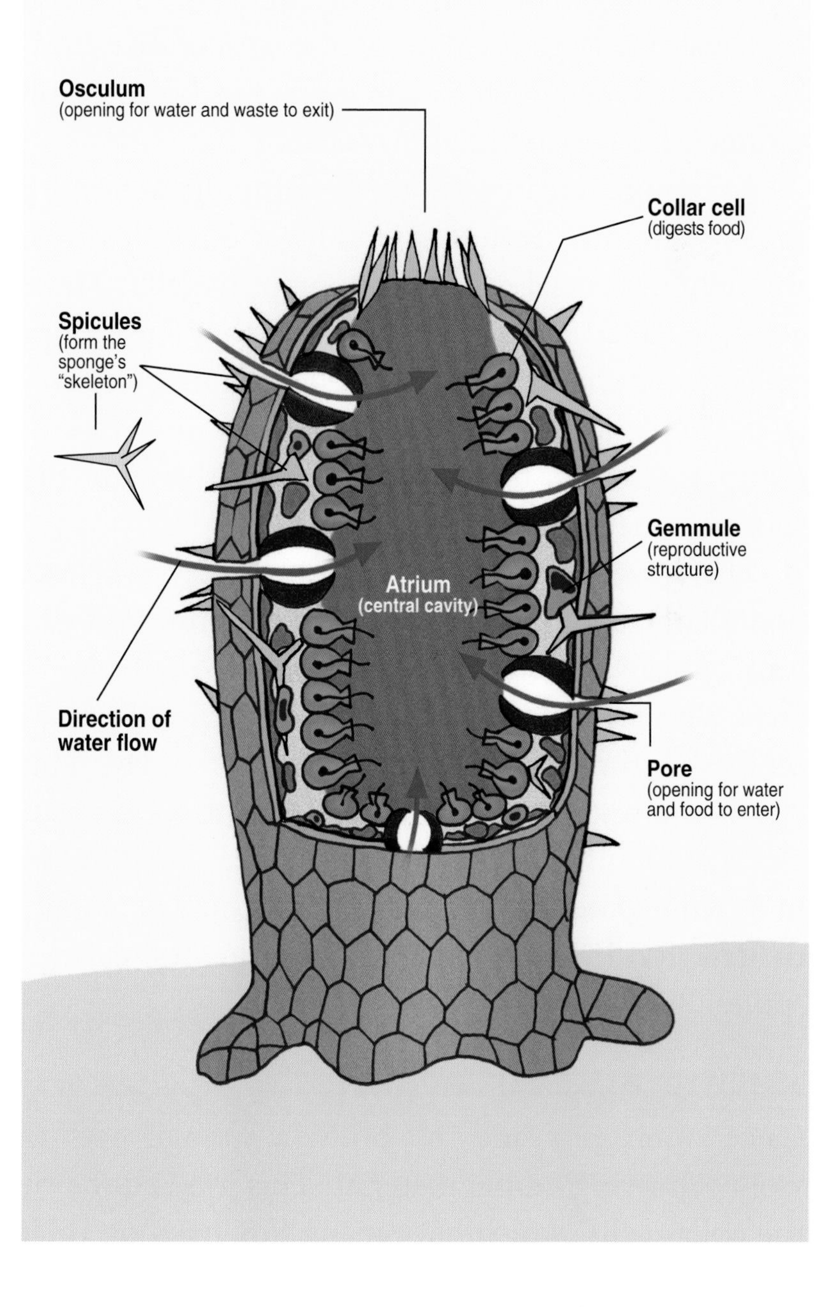
Anatomy of a Simple Sponge
Osculum
(opening for water and waste to exit)
Collar cell
(digests food)
Spicules
(form the
sponge's
"skeleton")
Gemmule
(reproductive
structure)
Atrium
(central cavity)
Direction of
water flow
Pore
(opening for water
and food to enter)

flows through a series of canals into a big central chamber. The water then leaves the sponge's body through a large opening called an **osculum**. Some types of sponges, such as the urn and tube sponges, have just one large osculum on the tops of their bodies. Other types, such as the grass and breadcrumb sponges, have many smaller oscula.

A sponge creates its own pumping action to move seawater through its body. It does this with the help of special cells that contain flagella. These cells are called **collar cells** because they have rings of hard material that circle the flagella like tiny collars. The collar cells beat their flagella inward, creating a current that pushes water through the sponge's many passages.

The sponge's pumping action is very efficient. Some large sponges can pump several hundred gallons of seawater through their bodies in a day. In areas with lots of sponges, much of the local seawater passes through sponge bodies every day. This cleans the water, removing most of the food particles it contains. For this reason sponges need to live in moving water that brings them a constant supply of new food. If these conditions do not exist, a sponge will soon die.

Eating and Breathing

Once water is inside the body, a sponge gets to work removing edible material. This job is done by the collar cells, which have many tiny hairs on their

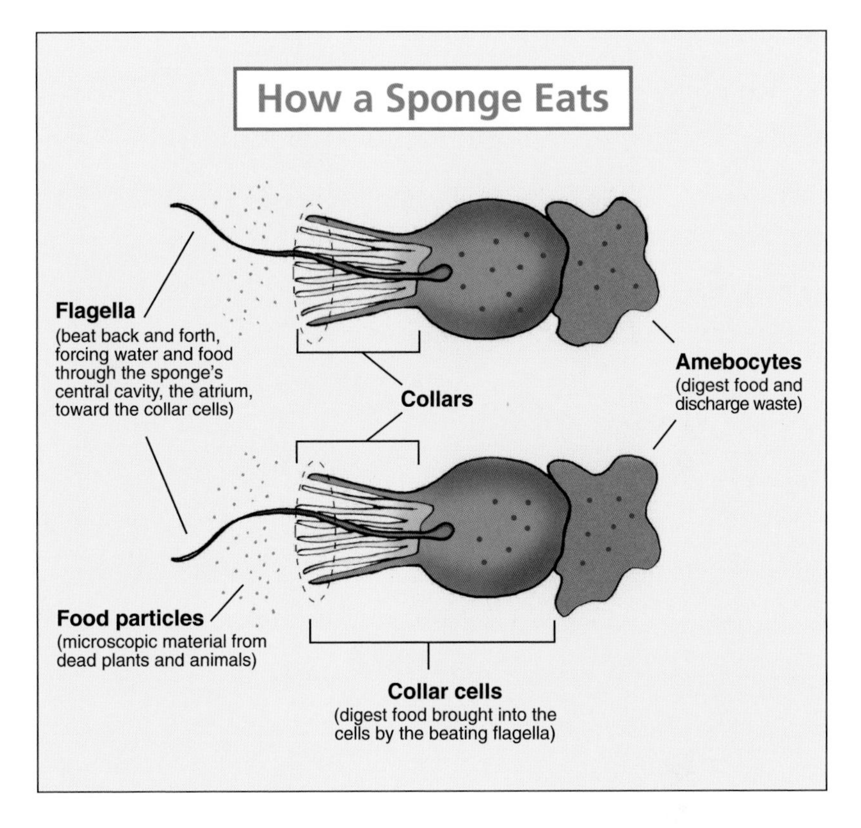

collars. These hairs snag bits of food as the water flows past. After being snagged, a food particle is brought inside the collar cell. The cell then produces chemicals that start to break down the food. This is how the sponge digests the things it eats.

Sometimes a collar cell does not digest a food particle. Instead it passes the particle to another cell called an **amebocyte**. The amebocyte digests the food. Then it moves into the spaces between the sponge's other cells, delivering digested food throughout the sponge's body. At the same time, the amebocyte picks up waste products. When the amebocyte has delivered all of its food and filled itself

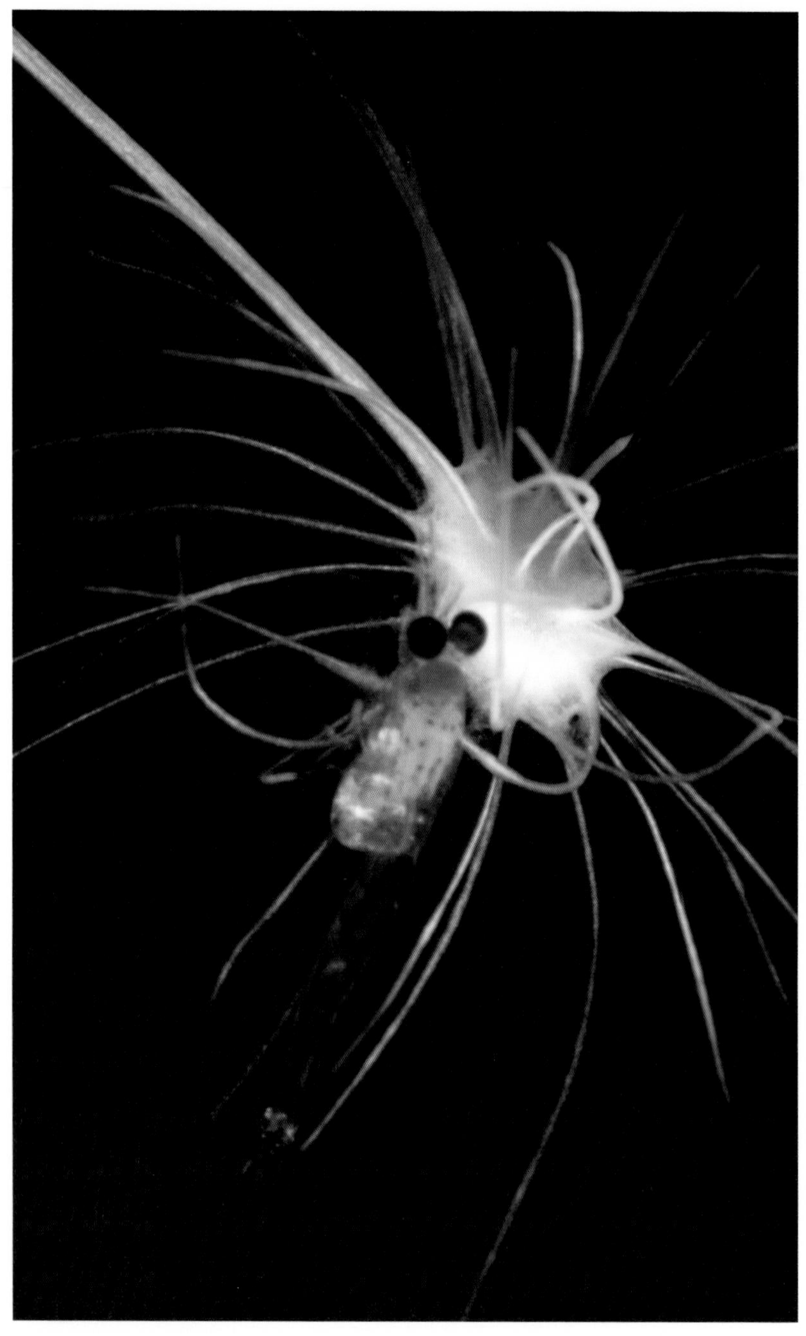

A hungry, white carnivorous sponge spears a shrimp with its barbed spicules.

with waste, it returns to a water canal. It dumps the waste into the moving water. Before long the material will leave the sponge's body through the osculum and return to the open sea.

Amebocytes are not just important in the eating and digestion process. They also deliver oxygen to the sponge's inner cells and remove carbon dioxide from the sponge's body. A single amebocyte can carry food, oxygen, and waste products at the same time. So for sponges, eating and breathing are basically the same thing.

Aggressive Sponges

Not all sponges are gentle filter feeders. Some are hunters that can capture and eat small animals. Sponges in one family, for example, have thousands of barbed spicules sticking out from their bodies. These spicules act like tiny harpoons, spearing shrimps and any other little creatures that come too close. Once the prey is caught, the sponge grows slender hairs from its body. Within about a day the hairs have wrapped themselves around the prey, holding it tight. The sponge's cells then crawl onto the prey's body and begin to break it down. It takes just a few days for the unlucky prey to be digested. The entire process takes place in the open water, outside the sponge's body.

Other sponges eat in a more typical way but harm their neighbors as they search for food. Encrusting sponges (sponges that grow outward in a thin layer) are especially well known for this behavior.

As they spread and eat, these sponges cover coral reefs, shellfish, and anything else that cannot move out of the way. Buried beneath a layer of sponge and blocked from sunlight, food, and oxygen, the encrusted animals soon die.

Nonencrusting sponges can also attack their neighbors. One type of sponge, for example, releases a poisonous chemical into the water. This chemical does not hurt the sponges in the area, but it is deadly to coral polyps. Polyps eat some of the same foods sponges do. When they die, there is less competition for food, so the surrounding sponges have an easier time finding things to eat.

Sponges as Prey

Although sponges eat constantly, they are not often eaten themselves. Most sponges taste and smell very bad. Also, sharp spicules make many sponges unpleasant or even dangerous to eat, and a hard outer layer protects the softer innards of these creatures. As a result, most predators are not interested in dining on sponges.

Still, some animals do eat sponges. Hawksbill turtles and certain fish specialize in eating these creatures. Other predators that sometimes snack on sponges include shrimps, sea urchins, crabs, sea slugs, snails, and sea stars. Many of these animals especially like injured sponges. When the tough outer layer of the sponge is cracked, it is much easier to reach the soft material inside.

Hawksbill turtles are often found among coral reefs, feeding on sponges anchored to the reef surface.

To keep themselves safe from predators, sponges use a variety of defenses. Some sponges, for example, are poisonous when eaten. Other species, including the fire sponge and the brown stinging sponge, produce chemicals that leave a painful rash on the skin. Fish and other animals may try once to eat these sponges, but they usually do not come back for a second helping.

There is no doubt that poisons and stings are useful weapons. The sponge's best protection, however, may be its amazing ability to regenerate itself. Even if a predator eats almost an entire sponge, the remaining scraps will survive and keep growing. Sponges are extremely hard to kill. This quality, perhaps more than any other, is what makes these creatures so successful in the ocean world.

chapter

4

A Spongy Home

Wherever sponges live, many other creatures are sure to be found as well. Many animals make their homes in or on sponges. Sponges have even been called sea apartments because of the huge number and variety of creatures they support. Most of the time this situation does not harm a sponge at all. Some sponge residents even *help* their hosts by providing food, oxygen, or other things a sponge needs to stay alive.

A Busy Community

Most animals have solid coverings, such as skin or shells, that prevent other animals from entering their bodies. Sponges, however, do not. Water and other materials, including small animals, can pass freely into a sponge's hole-filled body. A creature that enters a sponge may come back out again, or it may not. It may choose instead to live inside the sponge, where it is protected from the elements and from predators.

Shrimps are one type of animal often found inside sponges. Once these animals move in, they quickly build bustling communities with hundreds of members. In an especially large sponge, a shrimp colony may be even bigger. A scientist once found more than sixteen thousand tiny shrimps living inside a single loggerhead sponge.

An arrow crab finds everything it needs to thrive on the surface of a glass sponge.

A red striped goby forages for food as it hovers over a purple encrusting sponge.

Small fish, such as gobies and blennies, may also live in sponges. Sponge-dwelling fish are long and slim and can easily swim around in a sponge's water-filled inner passages. Many fish spend their entire lives inside a sponge, getting their food from the water currents that pass through the sponge's body. They even reproduce inside the sponge. Some fish let their eggs be carried into the sea by the sponge's currents. Others attach the eggs to the sponge's skeleton so they cannot float away. The eggs will hatch right inside the sponge's body. The newly hatched fish may leave the sponge, or they may stay there and live with their parents.

Shrimps and fish are just two of the many creatures that live in sponges. Other common sponge residents include algae, bacteria, crabs, worms, and brittle stars. The smaller organisms live within the sponge's inner passages. Larger organisms often live in the sponge's osculum instead.

Paired for Life

Glass sponges called Venus's flower-baskets play host in a very unusual way. These deepwater sponges are about 8 inches (20cm) high and 3 inches (7.5cm) wide. Their skeletons are made of countless glassy fibers woven together, and their oscula are covered by strong, hole-filled plates. The Venus's flower-basket does not have any large openings on its body, as many sponges do.

When certain shrimps are very small, they enter Venus's flower-baskets in male-female pairs. They settle in the osculum and begin to grow. Soon the shrimps get so big that they are trapped within the sponge's body. They will live inside the sponge for the rest of their lives, eating and even mating there. They seem perfectly content in their glass-barred home.

In Japan, Venus's flower-baskets and their shrimp residents are sometimes collected and given as wedding presents. This gift symbolizes a union that will last forever.

The Perfect Shell

Hermit crabs also have an unusual relationship with sponges: They sometimes carry sponges around and use them as shells. This living arrangement begins when the larvae of certain sponge species attach themselves to a hermit crab's shell and begin to grow. Before long the sponge gets so big that it covers the crab's shell. This does not bother the hermit crab, however. The hermit crab simply leaves its shell and carves out a living chamber inside the sponge instead. The crab makes a hole in the bottom of the sponge so that it can poke its head and legs out. It can easily walk and eat even with a large sponge on its back.

Hermit crab sponges usually come in colorful shades of green, brown, or orange. They are found all over the world. Most live in water deeper than 65 feet (20m), but sometimes they can be found in the shallow waters near the shore. Florida's Gulf Coast is the best place to see shallow-water species.

A Clever Disguise

Sponges do not just host hermit crabs and other creatures inside their bodies. They also provide homes and protection for animals that never enter the sponge. Barnacles and sea anemones, for example, often attach themselves to the outside of sponges' bodies. Once attached, these creatures will stay put as long as they live.

Other creatures do not live permanently on sponges, but use them as **camouflage** whenever the need arises. The sponge crab, for example, uses its claws to snip off a chunk of sponge about the shape of its shell. It uses its rear legs to hold the sponge over its body, thus hiding itself from predators. In time the sponge may even attach itself to the crab's back, becoming a permanent disguise.

This hermit crab has carved out a living space inside the body of an orange sponge.

A creature called a frogfish also uses sponges as camouflage. In both color and shape, the frogfish's body looks just like a lump of sponge. A hunting frogfish settles down on a sponge that matches its body and waits for tasty animals to approach. Because the frogfish is almost impossible to see against the sponge background, it does not usually take long for prey to wander too close.

Camouflaging itself as an orange sponge, a giant frogfish waits for prey to approach its mouth.

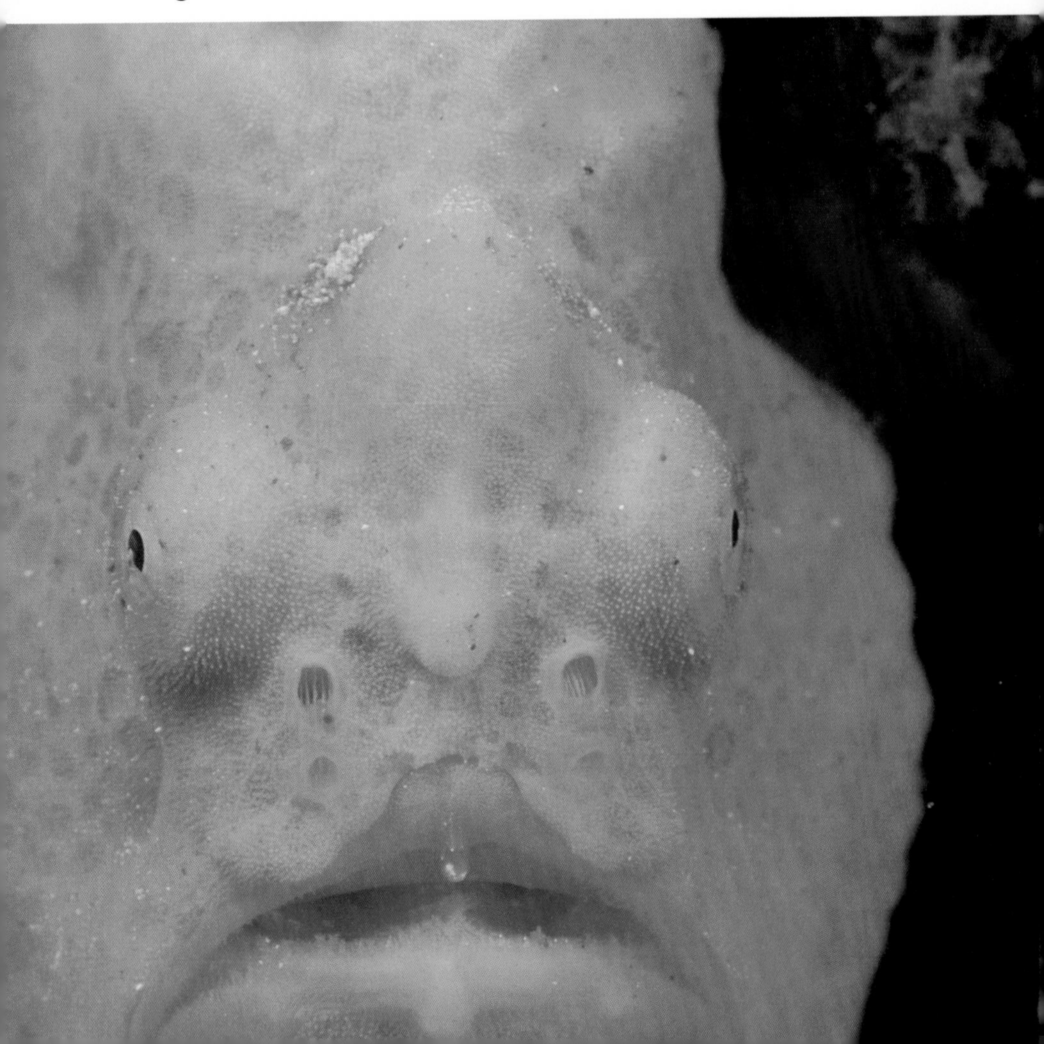

Hiding beneath a yellow sponge, this decorator crab is very hard to spot.

One bright red sea slug uses sponges for protection *and* food. This slug hides from predators by living on sponges that match its body color. At the same time, the slug takes bites from its host whenever it gets hungry. Over time, a population of these slugs can do a lot of damage to a sponge community.

A Good Arrangement

This situation, however, is the exception to the rule. Most creatures that live in or on sponges do not harm their hosts. Many sponge dwellers, in fact, even help their hosts to thrive. Algae and bacteria, for example, create waste products that sponges absorb and use as nutrients. Hermit crabs move their spongy shells to new areas and possibly new food sources, something a stationary sponge could not do on its own. And encrusting barnacles and sea anemones cover a sponge's body, thus making it harder for predators to eat.

Most of these arrangements are examples of **mutualism**, a relationship in which two different species help each other. The fact that sponges have so many of these relationships is part of what makes them so successful. The ocean world, after all, can be a very dangerous place—and when danger is everywhere, the creature that gets the most help is often the one that survives.

Glossary

amebocyte: A cell that moves around within the sponge's body, delivering food and oxygen and removing waste products.

budding: Creating new sponges by splitting off branches from an existing sponge.

calcium carbonate: A hard material that forms spicules in some sponges.

camouflage: Body features that help an organism blend into its surroundings.

chalky sponges: Sponges with skeletons of calcium carbonate.

collar cells: Cells that pump water through the sponge's body and digest food.

demosponges: The most common type of sponges, with skeletons of silica or spongin.

embryos: Unhatched sponges.

flagella: Tiny hairs that beat back and forth to create water currents.

gemmules: Small, hard packets that contain all the cells needed to grow a new sponge.

glass sponges: Deepwater sponges with silica skeletons.

hard sponges: Slow-growing coral reef sponges.

larvae: The name given to immature sponges right after they hatch.

mutualism: A relationship in which two different species help each other.

organic: Coming from a living plant or animal.

osculum: A large opening that releases water and waste.

Porifera: The scientific phylum to which all sponge species belong.

regeneration: Rebuilding the entire body from one small piece.

silica: A glasslike material that forms spicules in some sponges.

spawning: The release of eggs and sperm into the water.

spicules: Hard needles that form the skeleton in most sponges.

spongin: A flexible protein that forms the skeleton in some sponges.

Books

Elaine Pascoe, *Animals Grow New Parts.* Milwaukee, WI: Gareth Stevens, 2002. Explores how and why some animals of the land and sea are able to grow new body parts.

Maity Schrecengost, *Tasso of Tarpon Springs.* Gainesville, FL: Maupin House, 1998. Young Tasso stows away to Tarpon Springs, Florida, and becomes part of the Greek sponge-diving community. Winner of the Carolynn Washbon Award for Children's Historical Fiction.

Alvin Silverstein, *Symbiosis.* Brookfield, CT: Twenty-First Century, 1998. Discusses the three kinds of symbiosis: mutualism, commensalism, and parasitism.

Samuel G. Woods, *Sorting Out Worms and Other Invertebrates.* Woodbridge, CT: Blackbirch, 1999. Explains how scientists classify invertebrates, including sponges.

Web Sites

Animal Diversity Web, Phylum Porifera (http://animaldiversity.ummz.umich.edu/site/accounts/

information/Porifera.html). This site has lots of good sponge pictures and diagrams.

Introduction to Porifera (www.ucmp.berkeley.edu/porifera/porifera.html). Includes more in-depth information about sponge biology for advanced students.

Sponge Fishing in Key West and Tarpon Springs (www.divingheritage.com/keywestkern.htm). A brief history of the Florida sponge-fishing industry.

Index

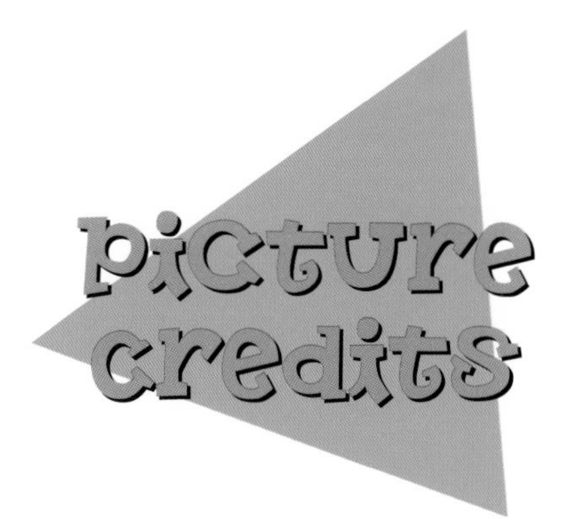

Cover photo: Michael Lawrence/Lonely Planet Images
© Hal Beral/CORBIS, 33
Courtesy of David Byers, 22 *(inset)*
Bonnie Jean Cardone/Lonely Planet Images, 39
© Corel Corp., 12, 15
© Eye of Science/Photo Researchers, Inc., 12 *(inset)*
National Geographic/Getty Images, 31
© Alexis Rosenfeld/Photo Researchers, Inc., 28
© Jeffrey L. Rotman/CORBIS, 8, 11, 21, 22, 37
Suzanne Santillan, 25, 27
© Marty Snyderman/Visuals Unlimited, 18
© Andrew Syred/Photo Researchers, Inc., 15 *(inset)*
Mark Webster/Lonely Planet Images, 5, 9
© Stuart Westmorland/CORBIS, 34, 38

about the author

Kris Hirschmann has written more than one hundred books for children. She is the president of The Wordshop, a business that provides a variety of writing and editorial services. She holds a bachelor's degree in psychology from Dartmouth College in Hanover, New Hampshire. Hirschmann lives just outside Orlando, Florida, with her husband, Michael, and her daughters, Nikki and Erika.